Losing Papa, Finding Hope

Belinda Anderson

Illustrated by Samuel Batley

heart
Pyschotherapy

Published in 2022 by Heart Psychotherapy Books

ISBN : 978-1-7397788-0-4

A CIP catalogue copy of this book can be found in the British Library.

Typeset in Open Dyslexic

Published with the help of Indie Authors World
www.indieauthorsworld.com

IndieAuthors
World

This book is dedicated to everyone out there who has sadly lost a loved one due to cancer

and to my lovely Dad

Just as you were

You will always be

Someone very special

In my memory

All proceeds from sales of this book will help to fund ongoing vital cancer research.

How to Use This Book

This book is designed to be used by a supportive adult, for example a parent, carer, teacher, counsellor or therapist to open up a dialogue in a sensitive way, with a child who has experienced a cancer related bereavement. It could also be used as a tool to help a child to understand the loss that someone else they know has experienced.

The key message within Losing Papa – Finding Hope, is to highlight the importance for young people of finding a way to manage and express their grief. As Papa Bear reminds Hope within the story, this may be through talking to someone, writing about how you feel, using art materials to express your feelings, or perhaps in other ways.

Whilst the story tackles the challenging, difficult and often harrowing subject that is grief, it also encourages young readers to hold on to the memories of the person they have lost. Through expressing our grief and holding on to our memories, we can learn to live without our loved ones, whilst they will always remain in our hearts

Hope was a cheerful, bubbly little girl. She had a loving Mum, who she called Mama Bear. She had a loving Dad, who she called Papa bear. And a loving brother, who she called Harry. To Hope, the world felt normal. She was happy.

Hope and her family did many things together. They went on trips in their caravan together. They visited her grandparents together. They had lots of laughs together.

But when Hope was nine, Papa Bear got sick.
'Cancer' was its name. Hope didn't know what this meant. But what she did know was that her Papa Bear was strong and brave. He would be better soon.

Papa Bear had to go away to the hospital a lot. Sometimes he needed to have an operation. Hope was always sad when he had to go away for so long. But she gave Papa Bear 'Lucky Duck' to take away with him. Lucky Duck would keep him safe.

Once, when Papa Bear had to go away, Mama Bear went with him.
Hope snuck Lucky Duck into Papa Bear's suitcase, she gave Papa Bear a
big bear hug and off he went with Mama Bear. He would be back soon.

Hope got to go and stay with her Aunt Jane. This would be good fun. Hope liked to stay with her Aunt Jane.

But one morning, Hope woke up with her Aunt Jane coming into the room. Aunt Jane sat on the edge of the bed. Slowly, and quietly she said, "Papa Bear has gone to heaven."

Hope didn't know what to say. She didn't know what to feel. What she did know, was that she desperately wanted to see her Mama Bear.
Very soon, Hope got to hug her Mama Bear. She couldn't understand why Papa Bear hadn't come home. She couldn't understand why Lucky Duck hadn't worked. Lucky Duck had always worked.

Hope felt everything was suddenly very confusing. Her world felt like it had been turned upside down and inside out.
Signs of Papa Bear began to disappear. Where were his slippers? Where was his knife and fork? Where was his laugh? Where were his big bear hugs?

Hope felt like a huge chunk of her heart was missing. She was lost. She didn't know how to tell anyone how she felt. She didn't want to tell anyone about the big hole she could feel in her heart.

Then one night, Papa Bear came to Hope in her dreams. Hope felt so happy to be with him again.

"Papa," she said, "I miss you so, so much. How can I ever mend this big hole in my heart?"

"I miss you too," said Papa Bear. "So, so much. Your heart feels empty now, but remember, although you cannot see me I am always there. Right there, in your heart."

But how do I make my heart feel less empty Papa Bear?" asked Hope.

"It won't be easy," said Papa Bear. "But you must always speak from your heart."

"If you feel sad, speak of your tears. If you feel angry, speak of your frustrations. If you feel happy thinking of the memories of our times together, speak of your laughs. You must always, always speak from your heart."

"What if I can't speak about my sadness Papa? What if I can't speak about my anger? What if I can't speak about my memories?"

"Words aren't the only way we can speak from our hearts, Hope. If we can't say them out loud, we can draw them. If we can't draw them, we can write them. There is always a way. But to heal the hole in your heart, you must find a way."

"Okay Papa. I'll try. I will try and find a way."

"And remember. Though you cannot see me, I am always there. In your heart."

"How will I know Papa?"

"You'll know. When you least expect it, I'll be there. Maybe you'll see a feather falling from the sky, or your favourite bird flying by, and you'll know I'm there."

Hope woke up with the sun peering through the curtains. She was smiling. She remembered the chat she and Papa Bear had in her dream. She felt happy.

As she walked to school with her friends, something caught Hope's eye.
She looked up toward the sunshine. Drifting down towards her was the
whitest, most beautiful feather she had ever seen.

Hope carefully grasped the feather between her hands. She placed it inside the zip of her school bag, smiled and quietly, under her breath whispered, "Love you Papa Bear."

Acknowledgements

I would like to thank my family and friends for believing in Losing Papa, Finding Hope from its earliest stages. For your ongoing support, words of encouragement and reassurance, I will be forever grateful.

A huge thank you to Samuel Batley who kindly agreed to illustrate the book for me, the illustrations of which are all beautiful.

To Indie Authors World, for your belief, advice and guidance every step of the way.

To all the kind and amazing fundraisers who made such generous donations towards the project. Without these donations, it simply couldn't have happened. I cannot thank you all enough.

And to my lovely Dad. My very own Papa Bear. Whilst losing him will forever leave a hole in my heart, I am eternally grateful that he had and will always have a place in it.

Author Bio

Belinda Anderson is an Art Psychotherapist and ex primary teacher from the Shetland Isles, with more than fifteen years' experience in supporting children and young people. In 2019, Belinda made the decision to leave primary teaching to pursue a career as an art psychotherapist, after becoming increasingly aware of the rising number of young people who required time and space, to work through emotional difficulties that may be distressing for them. Through her work as an art psychotherapist, Belinda provides a safe space for young people to express themselves creatively, using art as the primary mode of communication.

The idea for 'Losing Papa – Finding Hope' was circulating in Belinda's mind for a number of years before it came to fruition, just after completing her MSc Art Psychotherapy at Queen Margaret University in Edinburgh in the spring of 2021.

Printed in Great Britain
by Amazon